Original title:
Island Horizons

Copyright © 2025 Creative Arts Management OÜ
All rights reserved.

Author: Gabriel Kingsley
ISBN HARDBACK: 978-1-80581-623-2
ISBN PAPERBACK: 978-1-80581-150-3
ISBN EBOOK: 978-1-80581-623-2

Nautical Dreams and Moonlit Schemes

In the moon's glow, fish wear hats,
Dancing crabs play jazz with their flats.
Seagulls gossip, perched on a pole,
While the starfish try to rock and roll.

Mermaids giggle, their scales so bright,
Telling tall tales of the sea at night.
Octopuses juggle shells on a spree,
And dolphins join in for a splashy jubilee.

There's a pirate with a parrot in tow,
Singing off-key, stealing the show.
A squid in a tux, all dressed to impress,
Waving a flag that says, 'I'm the best!'

So raise a glass to the ocean's whim,
Where creatures delight in a merry swim.
Life's a party on the water's crest,
With laughter and joy, we are truly blessed!

Portraits of Light and Water

Splashing waves dance with glee,
Sunbeams tickle the sea.
Jellyfish do the twist,
Finding treasure they can't resist.

Seagulls squawk a silly tune,
Dancing round like a cartoon.
Shells wear hats, it's quite a sight,
Nature's party, pure delight!

Elysium of the Deep Blue

Fishy friends in bright parade,
Swim around like they're in a charade.
A crab plays catch with a passing shoal,
While a dolphin sings from the ocean's soul.

Turtles race with silly grace,
Waving to the clams, making face!
The sea is a carnival of laughs,
Where everyone's an artist with goofy crafts!

Sentinels of the Sunrise

The sun peeks in with a cheeky grin,
Waking up the day to begin!
Rays tickle clouds, making them giggle,
As roosters crow and wiggle.

Crickets hum in morning choir,
Toast bread in a dame's old flyer.
A rabbit bounces, wearing shades,
While a cat dreams of lavish parades!

An Odyssey on the Breeze

Kites dance high, pulling the sky,
Chasing after clouds, oh my!
A gentle breeze whispers a tune,
While children giggle near the dune.

Frolicking ants in a conga line,
While a lazy dog just reclines.
Nature's carnival floats so free,
As laughter rings in harmony!

Sunsets Beyond the Blue

The sun dips low, a clownish sight,
It spills its orange juice, so bright.
The seagulls giggle, they take a dive,
Sipping sunset cocktails, feeling alive.

As dolphins dance with silly glee,
Flipping fish like they're on a spree.
The beach balls roll, the waves just laugh,
A game of tag on the ocean's path.

The horizon grins, a cheeky tease,
Whispers secrets with the salty breeze.
Laughter echoes, a joyous tune,
As day bids farewell, beneath the moon.

Tides of Time and Memory

The tides waddle in like a goofy friend,
Pulling back with laughter that won't end.
Memory's a crab, scuttling 'round,
Pinching our toes, making silly sounds.

The sandcastles lean, a bit askew,
They wave their flags, a colorful crew.
Waves chant tales of the things they've seen,
Like a soap opera, in aqua sheen.

Seashells gossip in a hushed tone,
Whispering secrets, never alone.
Each tide's a jester, playful and spry,
Bouncing back, as the sun waves goodbye.

Secrets of the Coral Cove

The fish all sport their glittery hats,
Gossiping softly, like nosy cats.
Coral castles, a comedic show,
Tickling the currents with a gentle flow.

A sea turtle rolls on its back to play,
Making bubbles that giggle and sway.
The starfish wobble, trying to dance,
In a wacky rhythm, they take a chance.

Secrets hidden in the seaweed's fold,
Whisper of treasure, or stories bold.
But watch your step, it's slippery fun,
In the cove where the ocean's jokes run.

Where the Sky Meets the Sea

The clouds are fluffy, like cotton candy,
Drifting and dancing, looking quite dandy.
The sun winks down, a cheeky smirk,
Casting shadows that play and lurk.

Kites fly high, in dizzying loops,
Chasing the giggles of the funny groups.
While waves burst forth, a splashy cheer,
Tickling toes of those gathered near.

The horizon laughs, a joyous blend,
Where water and sky seem to pretend.
With each gentle wave, a ticklish tease,
Under the playful sway of the sea breeze.

Serenade to the Last Wave

Oh wave, you're quite the tease,
Rolling in with such ease.
You crash with a bubbly grin,
As I attempt to dive in.

You wiggle and splash, what a show,
Taunting me as I throw.
My beach towel flies high, oh dear,
Is it a wave or a sneaky deer?

Seagulls cackle, what a sight,
As they squawk with all their might.
I dance like a fool, you see,
Lost in a dance, just wave and me.

So wave, take my laughter and glee,
Wrap me in your salty spree.
By sunset, we part with a laugh,
Often, you're my tidal half.

The Journey to the Ocean's Heart

With a snorkel and flippers too,
I embarked on a quest, oh who knew?
The ocean's heart, so far and wide,
But here I am, along for the ride.

In my quest for treasures rare,
I tripped on seaweed, quite the scare.
A crab waved its claws with glee,
Saying, 'Watch where you swim, not me!'

I met a fish with a mustache quite bold,
It winked, and my story was told.
With bubbles and giggles, we made quite a fuss,
Turns out the ocean's heart's just like us!

So off I swim, with cheer and fun,
Collecting memories, one by one.
Though lost in the currents, I laugh and play,
For journeying's better in a silly way.

Echoes of a Sunlit Tomorrow

The sun smiles, a bright yellow face,
Floating high in the sapphire space.
I laugh at shadows trying to hide,
As tomorrow's echoes come to abide.

Shells chime like bells, such delightful tunes,
While crabs clap along under sunlit moons.
Seashells giggle, oh what a find,
Echoes of laughter swirl in my mind.

A jellyfish floats, quite the dancer,
It bounces around, oh the prancer!
With giggles and wobbles, it sways with glee,
A true artist of the salty sea.

As day turns to night, the stars play peek,
Echoes of joy, oh what a cheek!
With waves that sing of tomorrow's delight,
My heart leaps forward, all feels so bright.

Whispers of the Ocean's Edge

At the water's edge, I hear soft chatter,
The waves gossip, oh does it matter?
Seagulls squawk secrets, don't they know?
The best tales are where the tides flow.

Footprints in sand, a dance of the feet,
Where crabs scurry on their tiny beat.
With a splash and a giggle, I join the fun,
In the circle of laughter, no need to run.

The ocean beckons with its bubbly song,
As I wrestle with seaweed all day long.
Whispers of fun rise with foam,
In this silly paradise, we call home.

So here's to the beach and its joyful embrace,
Where sand meets surf, a laugh-filled place.
As whispers carry on, I grin with delight,
May the ocean's edge be my heart's highlight.

Reflections on the Water's Edge

With a splash, I met the sea,
The fish waved back, said, "Come see!"
They giggled loud, tossed seaweed cheer,
I slipped and fell, then cracked a tear.

Sun hats floating, drifting by,
Are they boats or pies that fly?
Seagulls squawking jokes galore,
I laughed so hard, fell once more.

The Language of Distant Waves

Waves whisper secrets in the tide,
I learned to surf, but fell with pride.
The ocean chuckled, made a splash,
I rode a wave, then met a crab's dash.

Seashells laughed beneath my feet,
They said, "Watch out! Here comes a fleet!"
I dodged a wave, slipped on a clam,
The ocean roared, 'Oh, what a jam!'

As the Stars Begin to Sing

Stars twinkle bright, they share a grin,
One sang out loud, 'Let the fun begin!'
I danced beneath, with sand in my toes,
But tripped on the moonlight, and down I goes.

The night sky chuckled, made a show,
Said, "Join our dance, but take it slow!"
I tried a spin, then lost my hat,
The universe giggled, 'Well, how 'bout that?'

Soliloquy Under the Milky Way

Sitting here, I chat with the breeze,
It tells me jokes that bring me to my knees.
The stars wink back with laughter bright,
I told one a secret, it laughed all night.

In shadows, crabs do the cha-cha dance,
I joined along, lost in a trance.
The cosmos rolled its eyes with glee,
Said, "Keep it up, you're funny as can be!"

Dreams Beneath the Palm Trees

Underneath the leafy shade,
A crab does its silly parade.
He thinks he's the king of the sand,
But slips on a shell, isn't that grand?

Lemons bounce on my head with glee,
Where did they come from? Don't ask me!
They roll and they tumble, oh what a sight,
I'll have lemonade by the end of the night!

The sun sets low, the drinks are all bright,
With parrots who squawk as they take flight.
A coconut falls, it's all in good fun,
Knocking down troubles, one by one.

So let's dance with the waves, laugh with the breeze,
Join the crab's party among palm trees.
With silliness bubbling like soda pop,
We'll party all night till our laughter won't stop!

The Stillness of Distant Waters

The water's calm, but watch that guy,
Fishing with a shoe? Oh, my oh my!
He thinks he's clever, a genius afloat,
But what he caught was an old sinking boat!

Seagulls circle, plotting their feast,
On chips left behind from a picnic at least.
"Is that a baguette?" one exclaims with glee,
But finds just a crust 'neath a jar of brie.

The sun lies soft on the shiny waves,
While jellyfish float like wobbly caves.
A splash and a laugh, then off they go,
Waving their tentacles, "We'll put on a show!"

So dive in and splash, be silly and free,
The stillness invites us to laugh with glee.
With jokes in the tide and fun in the air,
We'll sail through the laughs without a single care!

Songs of the Surfing Winds

The wind sings songs, what a quirky tune!
Riding the waves, shouting with moon.
A dolphin croons while holding a drink,
Sipping his soda and winking, I think!

The kites up above start to wrestle and fight,
Leaving the clouds fluttering in delight.
"Watch your tail!" one cries, as they dip and dive,
Come on, my friends, come on, let's jive!

The sun tickles cheeks, a golden affair,
As the grasshoppers dance, unaware of the stare.
In comes a breeze with a funky little beat,
The sand joins the party, tapping its feet!

So let's surf the rhythms, embrace the fun,
With winds singing loudly, and beats on the run.
A day spent in laughter, as goofy as can be,
With songs of the surf keeping spirits so free!

Echoes of Forgotten Shores

Footprints lead to treasures unknown,
Where seashells giggle, and barnacles moan.
A bottle rolls up and whispers a rhyme,
"Help! I'm lost in an ad for all time!"

The waves are a chorus, a splashy song,
Of flip-flops that did not quite belong.
A starfish struts with its glittery flair,
Saying, "I'm fabulous, just look at my wear!"

The sun is a jester, wearing bright rays,
Making shadows dance in whimsical ways.
A crab on the run takes a quick little stroll,
And trips over seaweed—oh, bless his soul!

So gather the laughter from forgotten shores,
Where silliness hides and the fun never bores.
With echoes of joy floating on the tide,
Come join the adventure, it's a silly ride!

Adrift in Serene Spheres

In a boat made of ice cream,
With a cat wearing a hat,
We row through the fizzy seas,
Chasing a fish with a spat.

Seagulls laugh, wearing shades,
Dancing on waves like they're free,
Dolphins surf like they're cool,
As they wink and sip on tea.

The sky throws a tantrum, bright,
Puffing clouds like cotton candy,
And the sun giggles out loud,
While the breeze feels quite dandy.

With jellybeans floating by,
And an octopus in a bowtie,
We toast with our fizzy drinks,
To the humor that fills the sky.

Elysium for the Weary Heart

Upon a hammock so high,
Made of spaghetti and cheese,
We sway to the songs of the breeze,
While eating ripe bananas with glee.

A crab in a flamingo suit,
Offers us lemon meringue,
While butterflies laugh at our feet,
As the coconut drums start to clang.

Mangoes fall like rain from above,
Each bite is a giggling delight,
As we dance with the fennel and thyme,
And the night spreads its magical light.

With a wave from a jellyfish friend,
And a wave from the moonlight's glow,
We toast to the silly moments,
In a paradise where joy will flow.

Castaway in Celestial Skies

Lost in a bubble of fun,
With a parrot who sings off-key,
We build our fort from old maps,
Dreaming of ships made of brie.

Mermaids throw us a birthday bash,
With a punch bowl of soda and spice,
While a turtle in glasses sways,
Telling tales that are rather nice.

Stars wink as they twinkle and tease,
Landing softly on our toes,
While the moon grins like a joker,
As the clouds dance in fancy clothes.

We feast on the laughter we find,
As the sun sets with a cheer,
With drinks served in coconut cups,
In a world where weirdness is dear.

The Dance of Light and Water

The waves wear disco balls tonight,
While the sun does the funky slide,
Crabs take their turn to moonwalk,
In this beachside carnival ride.

Splashing around with sea cucumbers,
We giggle at jellyfish doing the twist,
As starfish twirl in formations,
In this wild underwater mist.

Seashells whisper sweet nothings,
To turtles strutting with flair,
While the breeze tickles our noses,
Singing songs of the salty air.

With a firefly serenade near,
And the ocean playing the fife,
We dance till the stars start to fade,
In the rhythm of this wacky life.

Whispers of the Distant Shore

Seagulls argue over chips,
While fishermen doze in their dips.
Crabs wear sunglasses, striking a pose,
Making sure everyone knows how it goes.

A dolphin laughs at a sunburned guy,
Who tried surfing but just kissed the sky.
The lifeguard snoozes under the sun's glare,
Dreaming of sips from a coconut rare.

Soon the tide brings back a lost shoe,
It dances off, like it has stuff to do.
Shells play poker, the octopus deals,
While starfish cheer with all of their feels.

Laughter echoes, waves crash and roll,
As the beach becomes a carnival stroll.
Each grain of sand, a story to tell,
Turns the shore into a magical shell.

Beneath the Palm's Embrace

Under a palm, where dreams collide,
Squirrels share secrets, oh what a ride!
A couple's picnic with ants in a line,
Stealing their sandwich, oh what a crime!

A cat on a blanket, pretending to nap,
Watches for crumbs from a happy mishap.
The breeze brings a joke from a nearby kite,
Whispered so softly, it sparks sheer delight.

Coconuts grin at the coconut shy,
While sunburned tourists just pass by.
The hammock sways like a giddy little child,
In a dance with the wind, all carefree and wild.

With laughter and cheer, the day drifts away,
As stars peek out to join the fray.
Under the palms, life finds its pace,
In this quirky, sun-kissed, happy place.

Tides of Solitude

Waves tickle feet, a giggle escapes,
While jellyfish skip in their wobbly capes.
A crab walks sideways, in search of some fun,
Taking its time, not in a rush to run.

Lonely coconuts chat on the shore,
About ancient secrets and myths of yore.
The tide hums softly a lonesome tune,
As stars twinkle gently, like a cosmic boon.

A conch shell shouts, 'Join the clam band!'
While fish do the tango just out of hand.
By night, the moon joins the dance on the sand,
With laughter echoing, oh, isn't it grand?

Though solitude reigns in this quiet place,
Nature's antics bring a smile to the face.
In the tides of silence, moments align,
With humor etched in the quiet divine.

Sunsets Beyond the Blue

The sun winks at us, it's all in good fun,
Painting the sky with colors that run.
A hermit crab juggles shells in the sand,
While gulls make a ruckus, oh isn't it grand?

The children giggle, chasing the light,
As shadows dance past, taking to flight.
A boat filled with laughter sails out in style,
While dolphins perform, making us smile.

Cotton candy clouds float by in a whirl,
As fireflies wink, giving night a twirl.
The stars come to play in evening's embrace,
Creating a canvas of joy and of grace.

So here we gather, beneath evening's hue,
With stories to share and dreams to imbue.
In the glow of the twilight, our hearts want to sing,
For sunsets beyond, such joy they can bring.

The Unseen Path of the Horizon

There once was a boat made of cheese,
It sailed on the breeze with such ease.
The captain a cat, quite the sight,
Meowed at the fish, then took flight.

The horizon waved back like a friend,
Inviting the crew towards the bend.
With seagulls as guides in a twist,
They danced with the waves, never missed.

Then came a whale, wearing a hat,
Who joked with the crew about that.
"Why sail across waters so blue?
Just dive in, swim over—oh, boo!"

They laughed at their folly, so grand,
As the cheese boat kept sinking in sand.
But dreams hold no bounds, you will find,
Even cheese can float if you're kind.

Harmony in Chasing Currents

Two ducks in a pond did conspire,
To chase down the waves with a choir.
Quacking in rhythms, they played,
With a splash and a giggle, they swayed.

A turtle rolled by with a grin,
"You quack like you're trying to win!"
They flapped their wings, oh so bold,
While sharing sweet tales to be told.

The sun had a melt of bright gold,
As laughter bubbled from both young and old.
"Let's race with the wind, not with pride!"
And off they all went; what a ride!

In the end, though the race was quite silly,
They basked in the joy, feeling frilly.
For life is a waddle, a chase and a cheer,
With friends by your side, there's nothing to fear.

The Fragrance of Sunset Blooms

A flower once danced in the dusk,
Wore petals of gold, quite robust.
It called all the bees for a ball,
Promising nectar, the sweetest of all.

The sun wore sunglasses, quite proud,
As the moon peeked out from a cloud.
Together they laughed at the night,
With blossoms that twinkled, what a sight!

The breeze brought in scents from afar,
As critters spun tales of a star.
With laughter and pollen, they played,
In a circus of colors, they swayed.

When dusk turned to night, oh so bright,
The flowers still giggled in flight.
And though they would close with a sigh,
Tomorrow they'd bloom and reach for the sky.

Reflections in a Tea-Stained Sky

A teacup that floated high above,
Sipped clouds like a sweet turtle dove.
It spilled little drops like confetti,
Creating a dance for the spaghetti!

The sun, feeling fancy and spry,
Wore a top hat as it splashed by.
The moon called out, "Let's have some fun!"
And stars joined the party one by one.

A raccoon who fancied himself wise,
Wore glasses and squinted at the skies.
"Why not brew dreams in this brew?"
He poured out stories, much too few.

With laughter and chaos in tow,
They spun a tale that only they know.
In a teacup, so merry and spry,
Reflections of joy filled the sky.

Currents of Time Beyond the Reef

Fish in bow ties, they swim with flair,
Sipping seaweed tea without a care.
Time drifts lazily, like a jellyfish,
Every wink and wave makes quite the dish.

Coral crabs dance, they throw a ball,
Scuttle across the sand, do they trip? Not at all!
Tickling the tide with a playful twist,
In this underwater world, you simply can't miss.

The starfish giggles, it's quite the prank,
Winking at swimmers while they sank.
Life's a party below the blue,
With laughter echoing, just for you!

So grab your snorkel and join the fun,
Undersea shenanigans, never done.
Currents of laughter, they roll and flow,
In this sea of humor, come take a bow!

Shadows of Destiny on the Sea

A crab in a cape, what a sight to see,
Strolling on sand with all of his glee.
Moonlight dances on waves like a show,
Even the seaweed puts on a glow!

Dolphins wearing hats, a nautical troupe,
Throwing a party in a fishy loop.
Jellyfish juggle with grace and ease,
While scooping their snacks with a hint of cheese.

Seagulls are clowns, they squawk and they dive,
Dressed up in feathers, they feel so alive.
The ocean's a stage, and the waves have a laugh,
As each salty sprite takes a bow in the surf.

So fear not the deep with its strange masquerade,
Join in the antics, you'll never feel weighed.
Shadows may dance, but the joy is so bright,
On this stage of the sea, everything feels right!

Dreams Carried by the Sea Breeze

A tale of the gulls and their wobbly land,
Dancing through breezes, not quite as planned.
With sandwiches flying, what a comical sight,
They swipe them from picnics, always take flight!

The otters are plotting a lunchtime feast,
Floating on backs, they laugh with the least.
Shellfish in tuxedos, all dressed to the nines,
Play charades with the tide, with no bad lines!

Whales with sunglasses sing tunes of delight,
Harmonizing waves with a laugh in their might.
The playful sea breeze whispers silly dreams,
As crabs share their secrets in chuckle-filled streams.

So let your worries float far out to sea,
In this world of giggles, come join the spree.
Dreams carried lightly, like feathers on tide,
With laughter and joy, in this dance we glide!

A Palette of Colors at Dusk

Crayons and fish paint the water so bright,
Splashes of oranges and pinks take flight.
Starfish with brushes, creating their art,
Each wave a canvas, a jovial heart.

The sunset giggles, it tickles the sky,
As clam shells chuckle, they flutter and fly.
Colorful octopuses wrap 'round the sun,
Creating a masterpiece, oh what fun!

Sea turtles giggle, as waves comb their shells,
Reflecting the hues where laughter dwells.
Bubbles like balloons rise up to the air,
Each popping giggle shows color's fair share.

So come and create with the ocean so free,
With brushes of laughter and shades of spree.
A world of bright colors invites you to play,
In this whimsical landscape, joy leads the way!

The Odyssey of Forgotten Shores

Once sailed a crab with a big hat,
He danced on sand like a chubby cat.
Seagulls laughed at his silly prance,
While fish waved fins in a fishy dance.

A turtle lost, with a map upside down,
Asked a starfish why he wore a frown.
Together they searched for the last piece of pie,
But all they found was a puffin's goodbye.

A clam told tales of a golden shoe,
Sworn by a mermaid to be quite the boo.
They chased a wave that just rolled on by,
And took a selfie with a passing fry.

When waves would crash, they would giggle and cheer,
For in their hearts, they held no fear.
Each splash and giggle rang loud and clear,
In the land where fun's the only frontier.

Nature's Breath at Water's Edge

A frog in a hammock sips minty tea,
While a raccoon plays chess with a bumblebee.
The logs hold meetings, dermestid with pride,
As the sun paints smiles across the tide.

The waves whisper secrets to the shores,
While shells gather gossip like nature's stores.
I saw a snail race with an eager fly,
But both got sidetracked by a passing pie.

A heron strutted in shoes made of reeds,
Trying to impress the gossiping weeds.
They laughed so loud, the lilies would sway,
While turtles played tag in their slow, cute way.

Fresh breezes blowing with playful delight,
Bringing new tales in the shimmering light.
Nature's own theater on the sands so grand,
Where every laugh echoes across the land.

Whimsical Wishes in the Twilight

At dusk, a rabbit wore a tiny crown,
He hopped through fields, never wore a frown.
Wishing on stars with a biscuit in hand,
He dreamt of adventures in a jello land.

A duckling quacked out a curious tune,
While an owl juggled under the light of the moon.
Both pondered wishes, oh so absurd,
Like flying pigs or a dancing big bird.

In the twilight air filled with magical flakes,
The fireflies challenged the night to a race.
They twinkled and tangled in a merry chase,
Underneath the night's gentle embrace.

Just before sleep, they giggled and sighed,
With dreams of nonsense tucked close inside.
For in their world of twilight hues,
Every laugh and wish would abundantly fuse.

Palette of the Setting Sun

A crab with brushes painted the skies,
While jellyfish twirled with sparkly ties.
The horizon blushed in shades of grape,
As dolphins practiced their broadway escape.

With splashes of orange and hints of lime,
They crafted a sunset that danced in time.
The flip-flops strummed to a beachy song,
While the waves clapped along, singing along.

A clumsy pelican dropped paint down below,
Creating a masterpiece, quite the show.
A beach ball rolled in to steal the scene,
As everyone cheered for the colors so keen.

When the stars blinked in with a bright, cheeky flair,
They held a contest on who could stare.
With laughter and joy painting smiles all around,
In this whimsical world where fun could be found.

A Journey to Solitude's Haven

Setting sail on a rubber duck,
With snacks in tow, we're in for luck.
Waves whisper secrets, fish wear ties,
Seagulls chirp jokes beneath blue skies.

We met a crab who played guitar,
Told tales of sandcastles and a falling star.
Laughter echoed through the frothy foam,
In this funny world, we found our home.

Palm trees dancing, a conga line,
Trying to keep up—oh, how divine!
Getting lost in the coconut grove,
Where every twist hides another dope.

As the sun set with a wink and grin,
We toasted marshmallows to a cheeky win.
On this quirky quest, with spirits high,
Who knew that solitude could make us fly?

Reflections on the Turquoise Tide

The water sparkles, like my cousin's teeth,
As he dives in headfirst, what a sight beneath!
Fish wear sunglasses, sunbathing with flair,
Making waves while we flounder in the air.

A pelican somersaults, what a clumsy joke,
While we try to balance on a floating yoke.
The horizon giggles, a sneaky tease,
As we pretend our swims are as smooth as the breeze.

Drifting on floats, shaped like a slice,
Splashing about, everything is nice.
Our laughter rings out over the sparkling sea,
In this vibrant chaos, we just want to be.

At sunset, the colors join in a huge fight,
Making the sky look so silly and bright.
With ice cream cones and sticky hands,
Funny memories made in these sandy lands.

Sheltered by the Sunlit Waves

We built a raft from jellybeans,
It sunk quite fast, oh what could this mean?
The dolphins laughed, they joined our game,
Chasing jellybeans, oh what a claim!

Bob the octopus tossed us a ball,
With eight long arms, he was having a brawl.
We cheered him on, our cheers went wide,
While he spun around with immense pride.

Sunlight danced on each playful crest,
Whispered to us that we were the best.
As crabs in tuxedos waltzed on the shore,
We dreamt of adventures and giggled for more.

At twilight, we feasted on grilled sea snails,
Singing sea shanties, spinning our tales.
With each wave that splashed, we felt so brave,
Who knew silly moments could make us rave?

Paths to Uncharted Dreams

Strolling paths made of candy canes,
We tripped on gumdrops, dodging sweet trains.
A parrot named Chuck squawked out old songs,
While we danced like fools, looking just wrong.

The horizon rolled out a striped carpet,
We slipped and slid like a cartoon target.
With jellyfish painting on quirky jams,
We became artists with brightness in clams.

Bouncing beach balls made from bright fluff,
Dodging waves that just couldn't get enough.
We called to mermaids who laughed with glee,
Oh, to be silly and totally free!

As the stars began to twinkle and glow,
We giggled and cheered, let's put on a show!
In this funny realm where dreams collide,
The paths we wander are our greatest pride.

Mirage of the Lost Land

A seagull wearing shades, quite the sight,
Barking at the beach with all its might.
Sandcastles that crumble, come what may,
Claimed as a fortress, 'til swept away.

A dog in a hat runs off with my drink,
As I watch sunbathers too red to think.
Surfboards collide, oh what a scene,
The lifeguard's a hero, or so he claims to be.

Flip-flops are flying, a rescue in play,
While a crab hosts a party, hip-hip-hooray!
Sunscreen wars break out, a slippery jest,
Who knew a picnic could turn to a fest?

The tide rolls in laughing, it knows the score,
With waves booming jokes from the ocean floor.
So let's raise a toast to the joy that we find,
In the silly moments that tickle our mind.

Echoes Along the Coast

Whispers in the breeze, a prankster's delight,
Tidal waves of laughter, oh what a sight!
Seashells tell tales of fashion so bold,
While the barnacles cling, refusing the cold.

The sun's a hotdog, drizzled in rays,
Fried octopus jokes about its lazy days.
Jellyfish dance, with moves like a pro,
While clams hide away, under the show.

Waves crash and giggle, they never rest,
Surfing otters fight, who's the best dressed?
Lost flip-flop treasures washed ashore,
Each with a story, each with a score.

As seagulls discuss who's the funniest bird,
I laugh with a dolphin, it's absolutely absurd.
Echoes of chuckles stretch far and wide,
Along the squeaky sand, we take it in stride.

Where the Waves Meet the Sky

A surfboard lies sunbathing on the sand,
Claiming it's tired from trips that were planned.
Mermaids are sunbathing, gossiping loud,
While fish jump up high, trying to feel proud.

The sky wears a tutu, clouds float with grace,
While the sun plays tag, warming each face.
Seashells are trophies for the best curl,
As sand fills my shoes, what a crazy whirl!

A dolphin in shades just did a backflip,
Synchronized swimming, a slick little trip.
Turtles move slow, but they rule the shore,
Who knew that they'd become dance floor galore?

The waves share a giggle, as they splash and retreat,
Like a headline comedian, oh so discreet.
When the horizon meets blue, laughter's the prize,
Life's an adventure, beneath colorful skies.

Secrets of the Hidden Cove

In a cove where the secrets giggle and hide,
Lurking sea creatures, on the fun-filled tide.
A crab spins tales of those lost at sea,
While starfish perform, oh what glee!

The coconut drinks, they've got stories to spill,
Shaking their heads at the pirates' thrill.
Seagulls play catch with a beach ball so bright,
As sunbathers snack, from noon until night.

A treasure map drawn on the back of my hand,
Leads me to trouble, all part of the plan.
Jellybeans fish tell me to swim along,
As the waves sing a sea shanty, merry and strong.

In this cove of chuckles, the fun never ends,
With fishy comedians as my salty friends.
When the sun dips low, and the stars take their place,
We'll laugh at the ocean, and its endless embrace.

Footsteps on Untamed Beaches

Sandy toes and salty breeze,
We dance like crabs on wobbly knees.
A seagull swoops for fries on the run,
I shout, "Hey bird, that's not for fun!"

The waves approach, a cheeky wave,
I dodge and dive, feel like a knave.
The surf's a clown, it pulls my shorts,
I'm laughing hard, forgetting reports.

Sunburned noses are quite the sight,
My friend's face is a tomato tonight.
He applies lotion like a paint job,
Screaming, "My back! I need some slob!"

Later we feast on shellfish delight,
A crab does the cha-cha, such a sight.
My fortune cookie claims I'm a star,
But I'm just a guy who swims from afar.

A Refuge in the Quiet Embrace

In a hammock hung with scenic hopes,
I swing and ponder ridiculous scopes.
The wind is sly, it steals my hat,
Up it flies, like a rogue acrobat!

The mango tree waves, "What's the fuss?"
I reply, "Just some whimsical rust!"
A lizard lounges, a sunbathing champ,
While I giggle at his sunburned lamp.

A coconut drops, it's anyone's guess,
Will it thud or prove to be a mess?
My friend fears it's a deadly bomb,
But laughs it off with a snack in his palm.

As shadows grow, we tell ghost tales,
Where the sun is a ghost and the sand never fails.
Laughter erupts, echoing the night,
Under stars that twinkle with sheer delight.

Echoing Laughter in the Breeze

Upon the cliffs where the sea spray glints,
I trip and tumble, showing my prints.
"Is this the dance of the playful gnome?"
My pals laugh, as I claim it's home.

We launch a boat made of cardboard and dreams,
It floats like my hopes or so it seems.
A seagull mocks as it swoops for a snack,
I yell, "Did you finish it? Come on, come back!"

Shells whisper tales of a pirate's spree,
But all I hear is my friend's cackling plea.
"Let's build a fortress, a grand sandy den!"
We end up with a sandcastle mess again.

Evening descends with starlit surprise,
The moon winks down, so cunning and wise.
We sing silly songs to a tune of our vibe,
While the tide rolls in, our laughter imbibe.

The Gentle Call of Faraway Shores

A sea breeze whispers, "Time to play tricks,"
As we balance on waves, avoiding the mix.
My friend is the captain with a parrot's hat,
The parrot's a rock; he prefers to chat.

The tide pulls back, a game of peek-a-boo,
Where splashes become our laughter's cue.
"I'm a mermaid!" I shout with a splash too grand,
But dolphins circle like they own the strand.

We build our dreams with seashells and sand,
I use too much glue, what a sticky brand!
My future's uncertain, it's melting away,
But at least I have fun come what may.

As dusk wraps the shore in a soft, warm glow,
We chase the last waves like kids at a show.
With giggles echoing across the night shore,
We'll treasure these moments; oh, who could want more?

Lullabies from the Gentle Breeze

A parrot sings a silly tune,
While crabs dance under the moon.
Seagulls giggle, take a dive,
As the fish play hide and jive.

The waves tickle sandy toes,
While sunburnt tourists strike a pose.
A coconut falls with a thud,
Creating quite the funny flood.

Dolphins leap with joyful grace,
Wearing tiny goggles for a race.
Beach balls fly, but who will catch?
The octopus lays a funny snatch!

With each wave, laughter rolls,
As flip-flops thrive in summer strolls.
Under this sky so full of cheer,
Every giggle brings the world near.

A Canvas of Dappled Sunlight

Painting shadows with a brush,
The crabs in caps make quite a fuss.
A sunbeam tickles the old pine,
As raccoons plot their lunchtime dine.

The pelicans preen in their stylish wear,
Swapping out tips for a smooth hair care.
A monkey sneezes, sends fruit flying,
While a toucan shrieks with no denying.

A beach party starts, with tunes galore,
Flip-flops clapping, always wanting more.
The ice cream melts, but smiles stay bright,
While sunburned friends laugh, what a sight!

With dappled rays and painted tricks,
Everyone's ready for some beachy kicks.
Under the vibrant, fun-filled scene,
We dance and sing, living the dream.

Beneath the Gilded Sky

Under a sky of golden hue,
The turtles play peek-a-boo.
A jellyfish floats, a floppy friend,
Making splashes that never end.

A hermit crab wears a shoe too tight,
Stumbling past as he takes flight.
The sun is hot, the lemonade's too sweet,
As the beach balls roll, life's a treat!

The sun sets low, a fiery show,
While kids chase crabs, moving slow.
A conch shell says, "You're in my way!"
Grumpy and loud, it has its say.

But as the stars peek out with glee,
The sandcastles sway, "Look at me!"
Waves crash softly, as laughter flies,
Under the blanket of gilded skies.

The Endless Blue Embrace

Blue and bright, the ocean sings,
While seaweed twirls like fancy rings.
A dolphin dons a funny hat,
While seagulls argue, "No, that's flat!"

The clams throw a party, under the tide,
Shells dancing wildly, no place to hide.
Around the rocks, the sea stars waltz,
As laughter spins, who needs to halt?

The breeze tells tales of sand so fine,
As crabs hold conch shells and sip on brine.
A fish swims by, wearing a grin,
While sea urchins blush beneath their fin.

With waves that giggle, and salty schemes,
Life here is bright with playful dreams.
In the endless sea, let's join the chase,
A carnival laugh in this blue embrace.

Beyond the Point of No Return

A sailor's snack floats on the breeze,
With jellyfish waltzing, oh what a tease!
The compass spins like a lost ballet,
As seagulls squawk their mischief display.

Far from land, we sip on our brew,
The captain's lost it, we're all feeling blue.
With waves that giggle and tickle our toes,
We wonder where this crazy boat goes.

A dolphin jokes in a bathtub of sea,
Saying, "Come on guys, just follow me!"
While octopus jugglers steal the show,
We can't stop laughing at their watery flow.

Under the sun, we dance with delight,
But sunscreen's a battle—we all end up white!
So here's a toast, to our nautical strife,
And the finest crew—a regular clown life!

A Voyage Through Radiant Dreams

We set sail at dawn, dreams twinkling bright,
With hats on our heads, looking quite a sight.
The wind howls a tune that makes us all cheer,
While a crab on the deck clinks beers with good cheer.

The captain thinks he's a chart-topping star,
While singing old sea shanties from afar.
But the map is upside down, oh what a surprise,
We're lost in the giggles and oceanic pies!

Mermaids giggle, pulling pranks on the crew,
Offering treasures—a shell or two.
We barter with laughter, a dance and a dive,
Trading our sanity to feel so alive!

Then the moon makes a joke, splashing on the sea,
We try to catch fish, but they're all just like me!
With forks and a laugh, we call it a night,
To the sounds of the waves, what a hilarious sight!

The Passage of Echoing Seas

On a raft made of laughter, we float with great glee,
With talking turtles that sip on fine tea.
The gulls tell us jokes, they're quite the wisecracks,
As waves tickle our feet, no need for a snack.

Our sails are made out of cheese and of dreams,
While sharks wear top hats, or so it seems.
They dance in the foamy, bold bubblegum tide,
Encouraging our folly, with joy they abide.

We raise our odd glasses in merry regards,
To the fish in tuxedos that play on the yards.
Each splash is a laugh, each dive is a prank,
As we float through the silliness, joy fills the tank.

Our journey's a riddle, a joke by the sea,
Where the waves hold secrets that giggle with glee!
So here we shall linger, forever and more,
In these echoing waters, who could ask for more?

Silhouettes on the Horizon

With shadows of laughter, we dance on the shore,
As sunburned jokes echo, we can't ask for more.
A piñata whale objects to our glee,
Declaring, "My friends, come play catch with me!"

The sails wave goodbye, a real comical sight,
As crabs play the drums on an old pot at night.
The tides tickle secrets in whispers so sweet,
While seagulls host parties, the drinks are a treat!

From sunrise to sunset, we guffaw and giggle,
Painting the horizon with quirky dribble.
Adventure's a friend that we can't seem to shake,
With silly calamities in each wave we make.

So here's to the laughter that binds us in cheer,
To silhouettes dancing, all drawing us near.
In this joyful journey, we find what we seek,
A fun-filled horizon, where humor's unique!

Lost in the Embrace of the Ocean

I thought I saw a dolphin dance,
But it turned out to be my pants.
They floated off with style so grand,
Waving goodbye, the ocean's hand.

With seashells stuck upon my feet,
I tried to walk, but faced defeat.
The waves decided to play tag,
In a game where I just lag.

A crab approached to check my shoe,
Said, "Buddy, these aren't meant for you!"
He wore my flip-flops, what a sight,
As I chased him in the fading light.

The ocean laughed, I took a dive,
Turns out that's where the fun arrived.
With fishy friends and salty zest,
I found my joy—who needs a vest?

Gentle Breezes and Starlit Evenings

The breeze whispered secrets in my ear,
But all I heard was 'more cold beer!'
I sipped and giggled at the night,
As frogs croaked tunes—it felt so right.

Starry skies above, quite a treat,
But I thought a seagull stole my seat.
I turned to chase, gave it my best,
Until I tripped, oh what a jest!

The gentle waves clapped in delight,
As I danced the twilight away that night.
With fireflies leading my funny parade,
I felt like royalty—unafraid!

A coconut dropped with perfect aim,
Landed on my head, what a claim!
I laughed and named it, "Sir Nutty," see?
Embracing the chaos, wild and free!

Whispers Beneath the Coconut Canopy

Underneath where coconuts sway,
I heard a monkey shout, "Come play!"
We danced around, a silly sight,
Until I slipped—what a funny flight!

A palm frond hat, quite snug and neat,
I fashioned one for my monkey feet.
He wore it proud, a royal king,
While I just laughed at the joy we'd bring.

Cola cans were rolling down the lane,
I thought, "What's next? A soda rain?"
The canopy giggled, the palm trees swayed,
As we leaped and pranced, unafraid.

But shadows crept, the sun said bye,
I waved to cloud shapes drifting high.
With giggles echoing through the night,
We promised to meet, come morning light!

Navigating the Edge of Reality

I took a boat made from a shoe,
Thought navigating would be easy to do.
With oars crafted from a pizza crust,
I sailed away—oh, was it a must!

Fish gave directions, quite absurd,
"Left at the rock?" My mind was blurred.
I followed a squid with a map in fin,
All the while hoping I'd find my kin.

A pelican perched, squawking loud,
"You're off course, swim back to the crowd!"
I tossed a chip, he took the bait,
As I floated off on my crusty fate.

The sun set low, painting skies in orange,
With goofy tales that I'd soon forge.
A night upon the waves so grand,
The edge of reality, not quite planned!

The Gathering of Seagulls

A flock of seagulls flew in style,
Each one wearing a goofy smile.
They squawked and dived for a discarded fry,
A seagull chef, oh my, oh my!

They took a vote on the best of chips,
With flapping wings and sipping sips.
One tried to juggle, a fish in the air,
Landed smack on a beach-goer's hair!

The sun set low, their laughter rang,
As they danced on the sand, a silly tang.
With each splash, they just couldn't care,
Mimicking humans with clumsy flair.

In the twilight, their antics would boom,
Filling the coast with a seagull's room.
They cawed of adventures and dreams that stirred,
Making beach days feel quite absurd!

Murmurs of the Southerly Wind

The southern wind whispers with a cheeky grin,
Tugging at hats and making them spin.
It knocks over cups and gives dogs a fright,
Doing its best to cause mischief tonight.

It carries the scent of sunscreen and fries,
Tickling noses with its playful lies.
"Dance with me," it hums to the trees,
While messing up hair like a teasing breeze.

It swirls around children just having fun,
Catching their kites, oh what a run!
With giggles abound, they chase down the breeze,
As it blows away worries, with perfect ease.

Grains of sand caught in its playful hold,
The wind writes stories, both funny and bold.
In the night sky, it sings a sweet tune,
Tickling laughter beneath the moon.

Somewhere Between Sky and Tide

There's a place where the waves frolic high,
And seaweed dances to a jellyfish sigh.
The gulls cast shadows, looking for lunch,
While crabs hold a party, packed in a bunch.

It's where the horizon turns peachy and blue,
And sunbathers claim spots like sticky goo.
"Don't move!" yells a kid with a bucket and spade,
As the tide creeps closer; oh, the memories made!

The clouds are soft pillows, light and absurd,
With fish swimming by, giving one quite a word.
"Belly flop!" calls a friend, taking the dive,
While seagulls gather, and hilarity thrives.

In this quaint space, adventures come alive,
With splashes and laughter, as everyone dives.
It's a funny old spot, not far from the briny,
Where moments like these feel dazzlingly whiny.

Salted Memories in the Twilight

As the sun dips down, with colorful glows,
The salty breeze tickles, everybody knows.
Forgotten beach towels twirl in delight,
Forgetting their owners in twilight's light.

A crab in a wig struts along the shore,
While children build castles and seashells galore.
Laughter erupts at the flop of a flip,
And an ice cream cone, lost—what a trip!

Footprints tell stories of the day's fun,
As sand piles up on a sleepy bun.
And seagulls laugh at a sandcastle's fate,
With waves rolling in, is it a party or date?

Under a sky that sparkles like dreams,
The ocean whispers quirky little schemes.
Salted memories brought to life as they play,
In twilight they linger, come back another day!

Secrets Buried in the Sands

Beneath the grains, a flip-flop lies,
Its owner searching with wide eyes.
Crabs hold court, sipping from cups,
While seagulls plot to steal their snacks ups.

A treasure chest, filled with old socks,
Prizes of summers, lost to the rocks.
Every wave a new chance to play,
As we dig and laugh the hot day away.

The sun beats down, we dance in the heat,
Building castles with jello for concrete.
"Hey, don't you touch my jellyfish hat!"
Yelled the octopus, who looked quite spats.

In the end, we find pirate's gold,
A shiny wrapper, all crumpled and cold.
It's funny how secrets can change the tide,
From lost and found to where joy can hide.

Tales of the Coral Kingdom

In the deep, where fish gossip and dart,
Lives a lobster who thinks he's quite smart.
He wears a crown made of shells and weeds,
And tells of all his fabulous deeds.

"Once I fought a shark with a piece of gum,
And sent him packing—oh, what a bum!"
His friends all laugh, rolling with glee,
As he boasts of adventures beneath the sea.

A dolphin chimes in, with a flipsy flop,
"I once danced, and I just couldn't stop!"
They spin and twirl in the ocean's embrace,
While a jellyfish crash-lands, just to join the race.

The night draws near, stars shine so bright,
As they gather 'round for tales of delight.
In a coral kingdom where laughter proceeds,
Everyone knows fun is all that one needs.

Fragments of Eternity

On the shore, we're making memories,
Noticing how the waves tickle our knees.
Scavenging shells that look like old phones,
Chatting with crabs, while we're building our homes.

A starfish tried to join the local band,
But found he just couldn't quite understand.
With a beat that's slow, and a groove that's stuck,
He twanged his arms—oh, what bad luck!

"Eternity's just a blink," says a clam,
"Tell that to my brother, who's stuck in a jam!"
They giggle together, the night growing free,
Laughing at how endless time can really be.

So we gather our fragments, both funny and bright,
Sharing our stories in the soft moonlight.
Every giggle and gasp written in the sand,
As we roam through the twilight, hand in hand.

Enchantment of the Dusk Tide

At dusk, the sea shimmers, a magical sight,
Seagulls are singing, and fish take to flight.
A crab conducts with a twig in his claw,
While the waves applaud with a gentle "rawr."

The moon grins down with a wink and a smile,
As sea turtles groove, gliding in style.
"Can you keep up?" says a shark with a tease,
While the clams clap their shells, eager to please.

The water sizzles, the laughter breaks free,
With a star fish jamming on top of a sea tree.
Sea cucumbers cheer, though most folks just stare,
"Is that a band, or are they just a flare?"

As shadows dance wildly in the twilight glow,
Our hearts leap with joy, moving to and fro.
Dusk tide will end, but our spirits will soar,
With shenanigans spinning forever on shore.

A Sanctuary in the Sea

The gulls squawk loud, they steal my fries,
While fishy friends swim with big, goofy eyes.
My sunscreen's a beacon, bright white and thick,
I slip, I slide, it's a comedy trick.

The crabs in their shells do a curious dance,
With pinchers and wiggles, they're off on a prance.
I chuckle at dolphins, they leap with great flair,
While I struggle to balance my beach chair in air.

Palm trees do sway, what a wild, silly sight,
Their coconuts wobble, just waiting to bite.
As jellyfish float by, they wave with a grin,
I wave back with caution, let the fun begin!

So here on the shore, where the laughter won't cease,
I'll dance with the waves for my daily release.
A sanctuary found in this salty ballet,
Where joy is the tide that sweeps worries away.

Veil of the Horizon's Light

The sun wears a hat of blinding gold rays,
While I trip on sandcastles, lost in my ways.
Bikini tops tug and hide from the breeze,
As I dance like a fool, trying hard not to sneeze.

At dusk, the horizon blushes a bright hue,
While seagulls steal chips, oh the feathery crew!
With each wave that crashes, I giggle and shout,
In this playful ballet, no room for doubt.

With drink in my hand, I'm the king of the shore,
But suddenly, I slip and roll over the floor.
Laughter erupts, and I'm soaked head to toe,
In this gleeful resort, where the good times flow.

The fireflies twinkle, like stars in the night,
As I roast marshmallows and let worries take flight.
I'll laugh with the moon, my partner in crime,
In a world of bright joy where we dance out of time.

Shadows Cast by Ocean Dreams

The shadows grow long as I chase my own tail,
While sand traps my toes, I begin to flail.
A surfboard awaits, but I'm stuck on the shore,
Waves whisper, "Come play!" but I tumble for more.

The octopus waves his eight arms with style,
While I'm tangled in seaweed, it's quite the trial.
My beach ball does bounce, then it runs for the sea,
I chase it with laughter — it's a fishy spree!

The sunset unfurls in spectacular hues,
As crabs throw a party in their tiny shoes.
Each flip-flop I wear seems intent on escape,
While I dance on the shoreline, a haplessape.

With treasures of shells, I'll build castles so grand,
Till the tide claims my work with a wave and a hand.
But in this sweet chaos, I find pure delight,
In shadows and laughter, my worries take flight.

Serenity in the Coral Breeze

The breeze tickles noses, hair swirls all about,
While I search for my hat, the one that keeps out doubt.
Coral reefs below seem to giggle and sway,
As I've lost my new shades — they're on a fish's tray!

The mermaids all chuckle, tucked deep in the spray,
As I dive for the treasures that glimmer and play.
With narwhals and turtles, we form quite the crew,
Trading tales of our mishaps, like slippery glue.

With laughter so loud, I'm sure dolphins can hear,
While I picnic on sand with my snacks full of cheer.
But ants join the feast, and I yield to their might,
As they march with precision, what a bizarre sight!

Yet here in this splash of both madness and fun,
With breezes that whisper, "We've only begun!"
The surf calls me back, for the day's nearly done,
And I waddle home happy, feeling just like the sun.

Mirages on the Horizon Line

Sunsets dance with orange shoes,
Seagulls sing tunes of playful blues.
A dolphin in a tuxedo prance,
Inviting turtles to a wild dance.

Fluffy clouds like cotton candy,
Mermaids gossip, all a bit dandy.
A sandcastle's tall, but wobbly too,
While crabs cheer on with a sailor's woo!

A fish in a top hat makes a call,
As jellyfish host a swimming ball.
Every wave brings a giggle or two,
In the sea breeze, life's never askew.

So let's sip coconut juice with a grin,
While squirrels surf on their laughter akin.
With mimosas made from bright seafoam,
We'll make these shores our whimsy home!

Serenity in Salt and Sand

The sun wears a hat that's quite absurd,
While crabs recite the silliest word.
A cat with shades lounges on the scene,
While seagulls plot for snacks, quite keen.

Flip-flops laugh, they trip on toes,
As beach balls juggle and mingle in rows.
A seashell offers wisdom that's quaint,
Whispering secrets every wave paints.

Bikini clads giggle, what a sight!
Tan lines telling stories of delight.
Sandcastles fall like dreams at night,
Right before the tide's frothy bite.

A sunburnt nose is quite the prize,
With laughter echoing through summer skies.
We'll dance till the moon thinks it's our jam,
In this paradise where fun's a slam!

Tales of Hidden Reefs

Underwater quests with snorkels bright,
Fish wear bow ties, what a sight!
Octopuses tell jokes, oh so sly,
While clownfish chuckle and wave goodbye.

A treasure chest filled with rubber ducks,
Pirate parrots squawk, full of luck.
Coral castles sparkle, secrets abound,
As merfolk dance in circles profound.

Sea cucumbers share tales of their plight,
While starfish strive for the spotlight.
In this hidden world, both weird and cool,
Every wave tells a story, a curious school.

So grab a mask, join in the fun,
The ocean's magic has just begun.
With bubbles and giggles setting the tone,
We'll swim through laughter, never alone!

The Pulse of Nature's Retreat

Palm trees shimmy with a rhythmic sway,
As sunset sprinkles confetti all day.
Crickets chirp in a jazzy grind,
While fireflies dazzle, never maligned.

A hammock hums, cradling dreams anew,
Banana slugs dance in a leafy brew.
Lizards wear sunglasses, so nonchalant,
Hiding from sunlight, a beachy jaunt.

Frogs serenade with croaks of romance,
While turtles move in slow, leisurely prance.
Nature's heartbeat is the sound of fun,
In this paradise where laughter's spun.

So let's toast to sunsets, the stars ahead,
With silly stories and giggles to spread.
We'll sway with the breeze, carefree and fleet,
In this retreat, oh so sweet!

www.ingramcontent.com/pod-product-compliance
Lightning Source LLC
Chambersburg PA
CBHW072130070526
44585CB00016B/1618